"Life is short. If you doubt me, ask a butterfly. Their average life span is a mere five to fourteen days."
Ellen DeGeneres, The Funny Thing Is...

"Our love went from fly to flower to butterfly, and it was meant to beautifully flutter, not sit still on a shelf like a trophy to be collected."
Jarod Kintz, This Book is not for sale...

"Butterflies are self propelled flowers."
Robert A. Heinlein

"He said that we belonged together because he was born with a flower and I was born with a butterfly and that flowers and butterflies need each other for survival."
Gemma Malley, The Declaration

"Hundreds of butterflies flitted in and out of sight like short-lived punctuation marks in a stream of consciousness without beginning or end."
Haruki Murakami, 1Q84

"Like a butterfly stuck in a chrysalis, waiting for the perfect moment, I was waiting for the day I could burst forth and fly away and find my home."
Emme Rollins, Dear Rockstar

"Some things, when they change, never do return to the way they once were. Butterflies for instance, and women who've been in love with the wrong man too often."
Alice Hoffman, Practical Magic

"You can only chase a butterfly for so long."
Jane Yolen, Prince Across the Water

"A fallen blossom returning to the bough, I thought -But no, a butterfly."
Arakida Moritake, Traditional Japanese Poetry: An Anthology

"I have butterflies in my stomach. I'm not nervous, I ate some caterpillars."
Jarod Kintz, Sleepwalking is restercise

"One butterfly wing reflected wholly in a mirror won't give flight. Let this be a lesson in love."
Jarod Kintz, Xazaqazax

"My thoughts are like butterflies. They are beautiful, but they fly away."
Anonymous

"But on paper, things can live forever.
On paper, a butterfly
never dies."
Jacqueline Woodson, Brown Girl Dreaming

"A flock of butterflies riots in my stomach and steals my breath."
Stephenie Meyer, The Host

"I knew I was in love because I had butterflies in my stomach. Also in there I had flowers, a few rainbows, and leftover unicorn from the bbq the day before."
Jarod Kintz, Love Quotes for the Ages. Specifically Ages 19-91.

"My lips touched hers, like two butterflies in the wind. Then I went home, cut off my eyelids, and I've been living in darkness since."
Jarod Kintz, This Book is not for sale

"Don't be afraid. Change is such a beautiful thing», said the Butterfly."
Sabrina Newby

"Butterflies better understand than you, the meaning of love and sacrifices one must make for their beloved."
M.F. Moonzajer, A moment with God ; Poetry

"The butterflies have flown away, like my ignorance and youth."
Eileen Granfors, The Pinata-Maker's Daughter

"The butterfly counts not months but moments, and has time enough."
Rabindranath Tagore

"What the caterpillar calls the end of the world, the master calls a butterfly."
Richard Bach

"They seemed to come suddenly upon happiness as if they had surprised a butterfly in the winter woods."
Edith Wharton

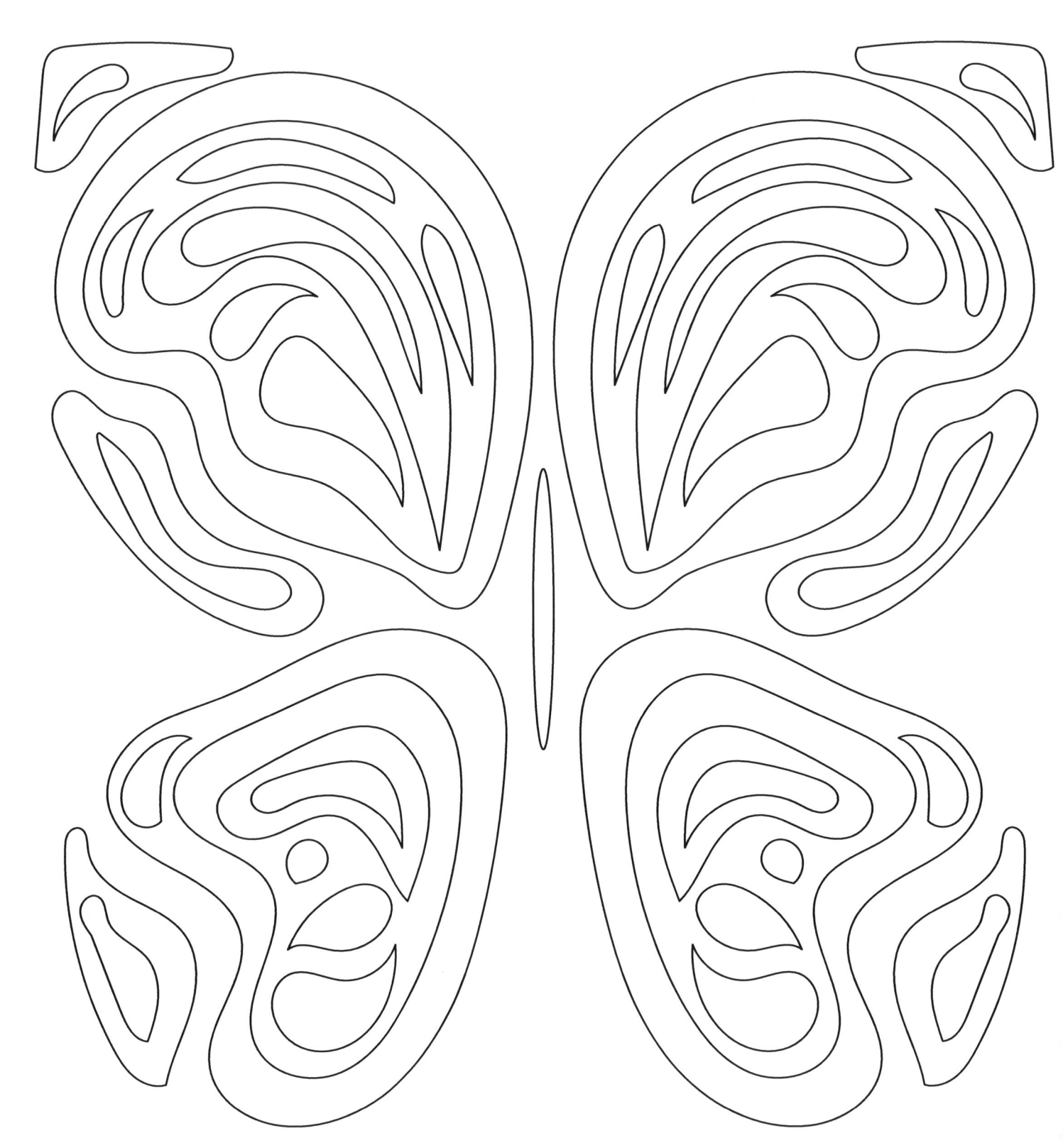

"Just living is not enough," said the butterfly, "one must have sunshine, freedom and a little flower."
Hans Christian Andersen

"Love is like a butterfly: It goes where it pleases and it pleases wherever it goes."
Author Unknown

"I only ask to be free. The butterflies are free."
Charles Dickens

"Flowers and butterflies drift in color,
illuminating spring."
Author Unknown

"We are like butterflies who flutter for a day and think it is forever."
Carl Sagan

"The green grass and the happy skies
court the fluttering butterflies."
Terri Guillemets

"The fluttering of a butterfly's wings can effect climate changes on the other side of the planet."
Paul Erlich

"I do not know whether I was then a man dreaming I was a butterfly, or whether I am now a butterfly dreaming I am a man."
Chuang Tzu